Nonprofit Quick Guide™

How to Find New Donors and Get Them to Give Again

Joanne Oppelt, MHA
Linda Lysakowski, ACFRE

Nonprofit Quick Guide: How to Find New Donors and Get Them to Give Again

One of the **Nonprofit Quick Guide**™ series

Published by Joanne Oppelt Consulting, LLC

Copyright © 2020 by Joanne Oppelt and Linda Lysakowski

ISBN Print Book: 978-1-951978-01-3

13 12 11 10 9 8 7 6 5 4 3 2 1

Printed in the United States of America

About the Authors

JOANNE OPPELT, MHA

Joanne, principal of Joanne Oppelt Consulting, LLC, is a seasoned rainmaker with a distinguished track record of success. During her twenty-five-plus years working in the nonprofit arena, she built or rebuilt successful fundraising departments at every stop, helping her organizations grow capacity and more effectively fulfill their missions.

She has held positions from grantwriter to executive director at the nonprofits Community Access Unlimited, Caring Contact: A Listening Community, Family to Family Network of New Jersey, Christian Healthcare Center, March of Dimes Central New Jersey, Prevent Child Abuse New Jersey, and Maternal and Family Health Services. Her extensive background in a variety of work roles and organizations enables her to understand the realities and challenges nonprofit practitioners face–both internally and externally. Her success at every stop positions her to help any nonprofit, whether through her books or consulting practice, turn around its struggling fundraising operations.

Joanne is the author of four books and has taught at Kean University as an Adjunct Professor in its graduate program. She is also a highly sought-after speaker and presenter.

Joanne holds a master's degree in health administration from Wilkes University, where she graduated with distinction. Her bachelor's degree is in education, with a minor in psychology.

LINDA LYSAKOWSKI, ACFRE

Linda is one of approximately one hundred professionals worldwide to hold the Advanced Certified Fundraising Executive designation. Linda is the author of ten nonfiction books, a contributing author, co-editor, or coauthor of twelve others. She has also written three books in the fiction realm.

Linda has more than thirty years in the development field. She worked for a university and a museum before starting her own consulting firm. In her twenty-five years as a philanthropic consultant, Linda has managed capital campaigns that have raised more than $50 million, helped hundreds of nonprofit organizations achieve their development goals, and trained more than forty thousand development professionals in most of the fifty states of the United States, Canada, Mexico, Egypt, and Bermuda.

She served on the Association of Fundraising Philanthropy (AFP) Foundation for Philanthropy Board and on the Professional Advancement Division for AFP. She is a past president of the Eastern Pennsylvania and Sierra (Nevada) AFP chapters. She received the Outstanding Fundraiser of the Year award from the Eastern Pennsylvania, Las Vegas, and Sierra (Nevada) chapters of AFP, was honored with the Barbara Marion Award for Outstanding Service to AFP, and received the Lifetime Achievement Award from the Las Vegas AFP chapter.

Linda is a graduate of Alvernia University with majors in banking and finance as well as theology/philosophy, and a minor in communications. As a graduate of AFP's Faculty Training Academy, she is a Master Teacher.

Dedication

Dedicated to all the donors who give generously, ask the right questions, and help change the world!

Contents

Chapter One

Acquiring New Donors Is Not About the Money

As our chapter title says, acquiring new donors is *not* about the money. "How can that be?" you ask. "Isn't the whole objective of pursuing donors to raise money?"

Yes, you are raising money. But money is not the goal. *Fulfilling mission* is the goal. Money is just the vehicle you are using. Money is converted to resources that lead to life-changing impact. Successful fundraising focuses not on getting the money, but on how donors participate in and experience being a part of making a positive impact happen. And feel-good, memorable experiences don't occur through the act of writing a check. They happen in the context of satisfying relationships.

The crux of successful donor acquisition is not going after the money. The crux of successful donor acquisition is forming and strengthening relationships between the donor and you, your organization, and your clients. And creating all that the word *relationship* implies—mutual value, trust, and respect. Where you both get *and* give something.

You Get More than Money Out of Effective Fundraising Relationships

So, what do you get of value? What you get of immediate value is easy: money. You get to meet your financial goals. You get to keep your agency afloat. And that's usually the mindset of board members, executive directors, financial officers, and operation managers. You may have that same mindset. After all, if the service system breaks down or can't be paid for, people suffer.

And that is where most nonprofits make their biggest fundraising mistake. Because asking the donor for money is like asking the donor to pay an agency bill. When was the last time paying a bill excited you? Well, it doesn't excite the donor, either. Even worse, treating donors like ATMs offends them. ATMs are objects. Donors are people.

Put yourself in the shoes of a bill payer. What kind of relationship do you have with your energy supplier? Pretty much none, yes? Our guess is you do nothing but pay bills and call them when you experience a problem. In fact, you might even complain about their rates, service, and billing practices. Is that the kind of relationship you want your donor to have with your organization?

There are things other than money that nonprofits want from new donors. For example, nonprofits want donors to say good things about them. They need advocates for their cause. How often do you sing your energy supplier's praises? How often do you advocate on behalf of their mission? How often do you even think about your energy supplier except when paying them or when something goes wrong? You don't. Is this the kind of mindset you want your donors to have about you and your organization? Or would you rather have donors who are willing to give, excited about your mission, say wonderful things about you, and advocate on issues that affect your operations?

Then don't ask for money. Ask them to make a significant impact in the context of a satisfying relationship.

What New Donors Get Out of Effective Fundraising Relationships

The key to getting financial gifts is by focusing on what the donor gets out of the relationship and making that experience as memorable and satisfying as possible. What value are your donors getting? Do they feel acknowledged? Do they feel respected? Do they feel appreciated? Are they making an impact?

The value for donors is a positive impact in their communities. The key is impact. The key to reaching new donors is focusing on their desires to make significant differences in whatever community issues are important to them. The focus is on fulfillment of mission. Mission, not money, motivates. And this is true of whatever kind of donor you're going after: individual, foundation, or business.

You want to make the experience of donating satisfying and memorable. You do this by acknowledging other people, most notably by listening. Are you asking them questions? Asking them about their needs and opinions and preferences and wants? Are you really listening to their responses? Actively listening, not formulating a reply. Do you offer feedback on what you've heard, so they know they're understood?

You also need to validate your donors. You need to let them know that they have value to you, your organization, and your clients. Saying thank you within forty-eight hours is a must, for starters. You also need to report back how the donation was used. And you need to regularly communicate to the donor about things other than donating. How often do you communicate with donors other than asking for money?

And when you report back, remember, they are not interested in how their donation affected your organization. Your board members and executive director are very concerned about that, but your donors are not. Your donors are interested in community impact. Communicate community outcomes to your donors as opposed to the financial ones you communicate to your board, executive director, finance officer, or program managers.

Respect and appreciate your donors. Make sure to thank them. Thank them more often than you ask them for a donation. Ask them questions and listen their answers. Let them tell you their needs, desires, preferences, and wants. Let them tell you what impact they want to make. Let them guide you in how they want to give. Let them know they made a difference and report back to them. Make the experience satisfying. Build a relationship that will last for years.

Focus on developing relationships and you will raise far more money than asking people to write a check. The process of relationship building yields far better results than anything else you can do.

Wrapping It Up
- The crux of all fundraising is in developing relationships.
- Mission, not money, motivates.
- Remember to ask for things other money that will make an impact.
- Acknowledge and validate your donors.
- Report back the community, not financial, impact your donors made.

Chapter Two

How to Find People Interested in Giving to Your Nonprofit

Whenever we are working with nonprofits looking to increase their fundraising revenue, we get asked, "How do I get new people to give to my nonprofit? Where do I find new donors?" Good questions. The answers lie in your focus on mission, your planning, taking advantage of all your community connections, the integration of your fundraising and communications activities, your level of engagement with your donors, and your follow-up. The more your message is about mission and not money, the more comprehensively you plan, how you capitalize on your existing community connections, to what extent you engage your community, and follow up with people who respond to you, the more successful you will be in acquiring new donors.

Donor Acquisition Step One: Stay Mission Focused

Be a mission maven. Individual donors are looking to impact an issue, not fix a budget. They are much more interested in hearing about your agency's impact on people's lives than how much money you need.

The ultimate goal of fundraising is not how many dollars you can get. It's about how many resources you obtain to make a positive impact. It is mission, not money, that motivates people to give.

The same is true with foundations. Foundations don't give money to nonprofits to make them financially whole, they give to nonprofits to make an impact. When you look to acquire new foundation donors, match your agency's mission with theirs. Be selective. Being selective will save you time in not preparing and submitting proposals that have no chance of funding. Your time is limited. Apply only to those foundations that are interested in your organization's mission.

A strong mission-oriented identity will also help you attract and be successful in garnering new business and corporate donors. A strong mission focus improves your organizational brand, something extremely important to the for-profit community. If you want to appeal to the business community and get top dollar, know your brand as expressed through your mission. Articulate your organization's financial and market positions while staying tightly mission focused.

Donor Acquisition Step Two: Engage in Comprehensive Planning

What gets measured gets done. As you are creating your annual fundraising goals and objectives, don't just formulate financial and participation goals, also include donor acquisition and retention goals. In addition to the activities you plan, write down the set number of new individual, foundation, and business donors you plan to acquire through each fundraising endeavor. That way, you can quickly assess the effectiveness of your donor acquisition efforts when the time comes to do so.

On average, it costs six times more to acquire a new donor than retain one. Donor retention is far cheaper than donor acquisition. It costs far less to raise one dollar through a repeat donor than a new donor. Yes, you need to acquire new donors. You will always realize some donor attrition and need to replace them. But don't acquire new donors at the expense of your current donors. The average first-time donor retention is an atrociously low 23 percent. That means, on average, for every hundred new donors nonprofits acquire, seventy-seven of them will not give again. If you're going to use all those resources to recruit new donors, it's in your best interest to retain them. The more you do to increase your donor retention rate, the more you will realize in overall revenue. So, have a donor retention plan in place *before* you acquire that new donor.

To retain donors, you engage them. Survey your donors to find out why they give. Design your donor retention activities around the feedback you get. Survey your former donors and find out why they don't give. And fix whatever the problems are. And always, always, always thank your donors for their contributions, whatever their contributions are.

Donor Acquisition Step Three: Look at Your Organization's Existing Connections

Donors need three things to be able to give to your organization: to be aware of and physically connect with your nonprofit, be it through a website, social media, email, or in person; the ability to give; and to be invested in your agency in some way.

Look at your physical connections first. Is your website easy to find and navigate? Is your website interactive? Is your mailing list clean? How often do you post to social media? Do people have a way to respond to you easily? Is it easy to give feedback? Make sure your communication and giving vehicles work, and potential donors are not frustrated using them.

Next, look at the people who are already invested in your organization. If they are invested in some way, they are a potential donor. Look at board members, staff, and volunteers who are already doing the work of your agency. Look at vendors and business partners who will benefit as you grow. Look at the business and professional associations to which you pay dues. Look at all your existing partners and ask them to contribute financially if they aren't already. Since they are already supporting your agency or the people you serve in nonfinancial ways, it is perfectly fine to extend the invitation to also contribute financially. They already have skin in the game. They already want you to succeed. Go ahead and tell them how you can be even more successful and make a more significant impact. Your increased strength will pay off for them. Make no mistake. Donors get something out of making a donation. Know what those benefits are and talk about them when recruiting new donors.

Are all the people in the above groups already donors? Then look at their connections. Their friends, family, and colleagues may not be invested in your nonprofit, but they are invested in the relationship with that donor. Ask your current donors to forward your email newsletters to their friends, family, and colleagues who may be interested in your nonprofit's mission. Ask them to share posts with their personal and professional networks. Have them retweet your Twitter messages. When you do this, don't always be trolling for financial donations. Use these vehicles to engage more people in your mission. Once there is some level of engagement, ask them to give financially. Build the relationship first.

Donor Acquisition Step Four: Attract People Interested in Your Cause

After you have recruited potential donors who have some connection with your nonprofit or its existing donors, turn to recruiting potential donors who don't have any connection to your agency but are interested in your cause. This involves spreading awareness of your nonprofit to groups of people with an inclination toward your mission.

Don't try and connect with just anyone. Try and connect with those people who will take the time to notice you. And for them to notice you, you need to be of some interest to them. This is why integrating fundraising and communication efforts are so important. Because to catch their attention, you must talk mission, not money. Yes, you need to make your appeals. But only after you have built some sort of relationship. And the beginning of a relationship starts with you getting their attention.

There are many methods to attract attention to your cause and position your nonprofit as a major player in the field. Your website and search engine rankings are one tool. Social media posts are another. Press releases are still yet another. So are speaking engagements. As well as coordinating or sponsoring a community event. Agency ambassadors are also common.

Agency ambassadors don't talk about making a donation, they spread the word about your nonprofit's mission and your agency's success in meeting it. Your board members and staff are agency ambassadors anytime they represent your organization to the public. Teach them how to be the best ambassadors they can. Give them the tools they need to successfully represent your agency. You can also teach existing donors and current or former clients to be agency ambassadors. Or you can hire a celebrity to be an agency ambassador. Anyone who can garner attention and speak to your mission can be an agency ambassador. Just make sure your message is clear.

To really make an impact, your message must be repeated again and again. Marketing research shows a message must be heard seven to ten times to be remembered. This means that your messages need to be consistent over time, across communication vehicles, and across people delivering the message. This is where providing an elevator speech to all your agency representatives helps. As well as speaking tips and answers to frequently asked questions.

Don't just train others on using these messages. Use them yourself! Use those messages in your grants and appeals, as well as your website, newsletters, and social media posts. Consistency, consistency, consistency. And remember, the message is about mission and impact as opposed to your agency and its programs.

Place your messages where people who are interested in your cause will see it. Use the communication vehicles they are most likely to respond to. Target your audiences. Go where people interested in your cause, your potential donors, are. Use your resources where they are most likely to have the greatest impact.

Donor Acquisition Step Five: Follow up, Follow up, Follow up

Follow-up is so important. When people ask questions, answer them. If you don't know the answer, find out, and get back to them. Collect contact information so you can follow up. Return phone calls within forty-eight hours. Give them answers to surveys they have taken. Tell them what happened to that petition you asked them to sign on to. Send them that financial report they wanted. And then engage them in dialog. Get their feedback. Say your message again. Impress on them the urgency of your organization's mission. And thank them for responding, whether their contribution is financial or not. *Build a relationship.* Once they're invested in your agency, ask for a monetary donation. And you will acquire new donors.

Wrapping It Up

- Talk about mission, not money.
- Plan your strategy and measure your results.
- Recruit among your existing organizational connections.
- To spread awareness, use consistent messaging, and target your audiences.
- Prompt follow-up is essential.

Chapter Three

Getting People to Give Again and Again

According to the Fundraising Effectiveness Project, the average overall nonprofit donor retention is 46 percent. That means that for every one hundred people who give to your nonprofit, sixty-four will probably not give again. And that isn't the worst news. The average first-time donor retention rate is a mere 23 percent. That means that out of every one hundred donors you've gained this year, seventy-seven will most likely not give again.

It costs an average six times more to recruit a donor than engage one. Do the math. How much money are you losing through donor attrition?

The Importance of Donor Retention

If you're going to all that trouble to find new donors, wouldn't it be nice to keep them? Wouldn't keeping the donors you already have, particularly your first-time donors, be a cost-effective fundraising technique worth investing in? If you spend six times more recruiting a donor than retaining a donor, which is more cost-effective? Indeed, the most cost-beneficial fundraising technique you can use to realize increased revenues is to improve your donor retention rate.

Don't get me wrong. You do need new donors every year as there will always be some level of donor attrition. You must recruit new donors. *But don't do it at the expense of your current donors.* When you develop your fundraising plans, make sure one of your goals addresses donor retention. And when you develop a fundraising budget, make sure you have resources allocated to improving your donor retention rate. Your fundraising results will improve. It's worth it.

So, how do you improve your donor retention rate?

Improving Your Donor Retention Rate by Thanking Your Donors

The first thing you need to do is thank every single donor for every single contribution within forty-eight hours of receiving their donation. Most nonprofits don't do this. Make sure that you do. It is common courtesy to thank people when they have gone out of their way for you. No matter what size the donation is, that donor is choosing to share their hard-earned dollars with you. They are going without something to donate to your organization. They need to be acknowledged and appreciated for that. The number-one thing you can do to ensure that donors will give again is to thank them.

And thank them a lot. Market research shows that it takes seven to ten times for a message to be remembered. That doesn't mean send out seven to ten thank-you notes. That means to thank donors through a variety of channels, over time. Hold a donor appreciation event. Thank them through handwritten client notes. Thank them through board phone calls. Thank them in your agency newsletters. Thank them at public events. Thank them individually and as a group each time you have the opportunity. Thank them whenever you can. You want them to know how much you appreciate them. Thank and thank again. No one has ever been offended by being authentically thanked too much.

And when you thank them, give them more than a simple thank you for whatever dollar amount they gave. As we talked about in **Chapter One,** donors are not ATM's who spit out dollars. They are people looking to make a difference, to impact a community issue. They want to know how their contribution made a difference. They want to hear about mission fulfillment. Show them how their donation was used. How much mission does their donation allow you to fill? A meal that fed a family? Five gallons of clean water that prevented disease? An hour of suicide prevention counseling that saves a life? Housing for a month? Medicine to twenty-five people? Ten pounds of garbage from a cleanup to help the environment? Twelve weeks of employment skills training that results in a job? Tell donors what they did. Use the word "you" liberally. Highlight impact. Focus on the human needs they met, not your agency's financial need. Just as in your ask, make your thank-you letters mission focused. If you want donors to give again, give them what they want. Show them how they are the heroes in making the difference they desire.

Improving Your Donor Retention Rate by Engaging Your Donors

The key to getting that first-time donation is to engage the potential donor. The key to retaining unknown first-time donors is to engage them in your cause immediately. The key to retaining your repeat donors is to keep them engaged. Donors who are engaged are much more likely to repeat and even increase their donations.

Start by engaging them in a conversation. Get to know your donors. Make your interactions personal. Make it a two-way relationship. Ask questions. Answer questions. Ask them to do something other them donate to your agency. Tell them the results of what they did. Give them feedback so they know their collective impact. Ask for feedback on how the experiences went. Ask them what is meaningful to them and act on their responses. Let them know how important a relationship with them is to your nonprofit—not in financial ways, but in ways the donor makes a difference in the lives of the people you serve. Talk to your donors person to person, through text and email, and in your social media posts. Communicate, communicate, communicate. Engage your donors in conversation.

Then go beyond conversation. Listen to your donors and respond to them. Find out what their motivations are behind the donations and structure experiences involving them that meet whatever is driving them to give. Don't assume what they want. *Ask them.* They may want to hobnob with other donors, maybe corporate donors or legislators. They may wish to participate in service delivery. They may want to meet a board member. They may want a leadership experience. They may want to learn new skills. They may want social experiences. The list goes on. Whatever it is they want, try and figure out how to meet the underlying need. Listen to your donors and respond to them beyond a simple conversation.

Once you start a two-way relationship, continue it. Ask donors to do something, like share a social media post, attend a community event, sign a petition, make another donation, ask a neighbor to join them at an event, or something else. Take the relationship to the next level. Then thank, thank, thank, and thank again. Start the engagement process all over again. Thank them, no matter what the contribution. Show them how they made a difference. Ask for feedback. Respond to their needs. Structure a meaningful experience. Deepen the relationship. Make the relationship stronger. Strong relationships with donors not only lead to repeat donations, but they often also mean more frequent and bigger contributions.

And don't always ask for money. Donors often complain that the only time they hear from a nonprofit is when it needs money.

I will repeat it: donors are *not* ATM machines! They are *more* than the money they give. Donors are people who want to make an impact. They have a lot to offer. Treat them as whole persons. Know their motivations. Meet their needs. Then they will respond to your requests for money.

Wrapping It Up

- Make sure your annual fundraising plan addresses donor retention, and your budget allocates resources toward improving your donor retention rate.
- Thank donors seven to ten times through a variety of channels over time. Show your donors the impact they made through their donations.
- Engage your donors in a conversation.
- Find out what motivation is behind the donation and structure experiences that meet whatever is driving donors to give.
- Continue two-way relationships that involve more than money.

Chapter Four

Building Relationships with Individuals

So, the question is, if you don't approach individual donors by asking for money, how *do* you approach them, so they give?

People are driven by values, feelings, and beliefs. They want to be acknowledged and validated. And they want to be part of something bigger than themselves. Appeal to the underlying values, feelings, and beliefs in your asks. Acknowledge donors' values and beliefs. What is the value in fulfillment of your mission? What is the payoff? Answer the questions, "How will I contribute to the greater good by giving to you? What part of being successful can I be? What will I get that is important to me if I give to you?"

We call this the partnership paradigm. We see it as an exchange relationship where each partner gives and gets something out of the deal. Each partner gets their own objectives met through the relationship with the other partner: "I have a mission. You are interested in mission fulfillment. Let me reinforce your values and beliefs by sharing with you how my organization's mission fulfills its mission, meets the values that are important to you, and reinforces the beliefs that you hold."

As a fundraiser, I know you want to feel good about involvement with my organization. As a donor, you want your behaviors, not only your values and beliefs, to be acknowledged and validated. You want acknowledgment that you have done the right thing, that you matter, that you make a difference. If I can do that for you, you are more likely to be satisfied with our relationship and more likely to donate again. People tend to continue in satisfying relationships.

So, I need to find out about you first. Donor research is key. Know donor values, preferences, and motivations so you can speak to their underlying needs. Put yourself in their shoes. Know the donors' perspectives and experiences.

Researching Donor Perspectives

Want to know what their shoes are? Research them. Know their general age and look up generational cohort studies. Two good sources are the studies by the Center for Generational Kinetics and "The Next Generation of American Giving: The Charitable Habits of Generation Z, X, Baby Boomers, and Matures," by the Blackbaud Institute. Then ask your donors questions through person-to-person conversations, surveys, or focus groups. Find out what they really think; don't assume.

In addition to checking assumptions, asking donors for their opinions validates them. When asked for their opinions or advice, people feel important, that they matter, that their voice counts. Listen to them and what they have to say. *Really listen.* What are your donors telling you that is important to them? What are they telling you about the quality of their relationship with your nonprofit? What is their experience when they interact with your organization? How can you make it easier for them, both in motivation and process, to communicate with you so their needs are met and there is organizational mission fulfillment?

Also, report back to them the results of what they did. Give them feedback about their valuable donation of time, talent, or treasure. Let them know they made a difference. Let them know what they did is contributing to what is important to them, that is, mission fulfillment. Do you send acknowledgment letters mentioning the value of the donation to the organization? Do you do it within forty-eight hours, while having made the gift is still fresh in their mind? You should. At the end of year, do you let donors know how their donation was used and what it accomplished? If you don't, you need to. Satisfy their desires to be acknowledged and validated. Give them feedback. Demonstrate how they made a difference. That's what will keep them coming back year after year.

Retaining Donors

Know what else will keep them coming back year after year? Letting them know you know who they are. Make sure the mailing addresses and salutations are correct. If I don't mean enough to you for you to know the most basic information about me, why should I get to know you and your organization? And, after all, if you can't get my name or address right, how in the world will you successfully manage my donation? Or, if I've been giving for years, don't I matter? Did all my efforts on your agency's behalf go unnoticed? Does my relationship with your organization mean anything? Not the questions you want your donors asking. Lesson: keep up the recordkeeping. It's more important than it seems.

You also want to send the message, "I and my nonprofit can be trusted." In your interactions, be authentic. Be honest. Be forthright. Your integrity is your biggest asset. Do what you say you're going to do. Communicate progress, including delays and failures. Address changes in circumstance, either theirs or yours. Communicate, communicate, communicate.

And, it almost goes without saying, when you interact with donors, always be courteous and respectful. People generally respond to other people in the same way they are approached and responded to. If you have the mindset that a particular donor is a pain in the neck, chances are you're not going to get a good response. In fact, the donor may see *you* as a pain the neck. Feelings on each side of a relationship usually mirror one another. If you have a negative mindset or feel that contacting a particular person is a dreaded chore, expect to receive that same reception. Conduct your donor communications when you are in a good mood and realize what an honor is to have someone take the time to interact with you and give of their precious, hard-earned money.

So, ask questions. Listen to the answers. Feedback information. Communicate almost immediately, often, and courteously. Know your donors. Know their values and motivations and appeal to them. Acknowledge them and their contributions. Let them know they are important. Make them feel like they are one in a million. And watch the treasure come in.

Wrapping It Up

- Acknowledge and validate people's values, feelings, and beliefs.
- Research potential donors and ask for their opinions.
- Keep your database current.
- Be honest, forthright, courteous, and respectful.

Chapter Five

Building Relationships with Foundations

I n the last chapter, we talked about how to approach and retain individual donors. In this chapter, we'll address how to build foundation relationships, shore up your foundation fundraising strategy, and get more donations from foundations.

Approaching Foundations

Like dealing with individuals, relations with foundations are based on mission fulfillment. And approaching them is based on successful mission fulfillment. Like individual donors, foundations see money as a vehicle to mission fulfillment. The question foundations ask is, "Where will our money best be used to achieve our legal objectives?"

Yes, I said *legal* objectives. Foundations are legally bound to the missions for which they exist. If they do not adhere to their legally stated purpose, they are at risk of losing their tax-exempt status. The IRS also requires foundations classified as private foundations to give out a certain amount of their corpus every year. Moreover, the IRS requires foundations to make their tax returns, called 990s, available—so that the public knows what they give money to and how they give it out. (Private foundations fill out a form 990-PF, similar to the form 990 that your nonprofit completes each year. For simplification, we refer to the form 990-PF here as the 990.)

In building successful relationships, there is no need to survey foundations the same way you would survey individuals. The information is already there. You just need to go through the 990s and match your organization's mission and needs to their requirements. Keep in mind, though, it is still an exchange relationship. Each partner gets its objective met through its relationship with the other. The nonprofit gets the money; the foundation is looking for successful mission fulfillment.

Since it is public information, foundations expect grant-seekers to read their 990's and be familiar with them. If you want to be successful in getting donations from foundations, start with knowing the foundation's mission, interest areas, geographical giving area, and funding range. You can glean all that information from the 990. A foundation's 990 can be attained by searching its website, asking the foundation for it, or visiting a library with a collection of foundation tax returns.

Of course, that's a lot of information to get through. It may be worth your while to subscribe to a foundation database that can search 990s by relevant categories, like issue, geographical scope, funding range, and others. Two foundation databases that we have found helpful are the Foundation Directory Online and Foundation Search. You can also use Guidestar.org to see the 990 for foundations.

Researching 990 should be part of a successful foundation fundraising strategy. Do your research before approaching any foundation. It's public information. Foundations expect you to know it.

Communicating with Foundations

Since foundations expect it, know who they are. In writing your proposals, make sure the names, mailing addresses, and salutations are correct. If the basic contact information is not accurate, and it doesn't mean enough to you for you to know the most basic facts about them, why should they get to know you and your organization? After all, if you can't get the name or address right, how in the world will you convince them that you can successfully manage a grant, financially or programmatically? The foundation will ask, "Will our money be used for what it's intended? Will we get reports on time? How do we know the information is trustworthy if they don't pay attention to what they're doing?"

By the way, do you submit clean grant proposals? When writing grant requests, do you watch for misspellings and grammatical errors? What about the budget? Is everything in the narrative accounted for in the budget, and is everything in the budget accounted for in the narrative? Is your financial and programmatic content consistent with itself? Do your numbers add up? Is your math correct? Check and double-check.

Details count. The most common mistakes are the sloppy ones, like errors in name, address, salutation, spelling, grammar, and math. Does your grant proposal writing process include proofreading and editing?

Remember, that although foundations and businesses are entities, they are run by people, so much of what we've said in **Chapter Four** about building relationships with individuals applies to foundations and businesses as well.

Your foundation fundraising strategy should also send the message, "My nonprofit and I can be trusted." In your interactions, be authentic. Be honest. Be forthright. In developing and maintaining successful foundation relationships, your integrity is your biggest asset. Do what you say you're going to do. Communicate progress, including delays and failures. Address changes in circumstances. Communicate, communicate, communicate. If there are changes in scope, let the foundation know *before* the end of the grant. No one likes surprises.

And, it almost goes without saying, when you interact with foundations, always be courteous and respectful. It's people who answer the phone, read the proposal, make the decisions, and report back to their board and the IRS. Like individual donors, people who represent foundations need to be acknowledged and validated. If they're exasperated and short with you, it means they're having problems they don't want to deal with. It isn't easy giving away money—everybody wants some of it and all the causes are generally worthy. It's not easy to tell a nonprofit that the foundation can't fund you. Be sensitive to that.

Bringing in the Money

If you do end up getting funded by the foundation, pat yourself on the back and shout, "Hooray!" Let the rest of the office in on the celebration. Everyone will be happy you brought in the money. Enjoy the positive vibes while they last. You worked hard, and your hard work paid off.

But this isn't the end of the road. Getting a donation from a foundation is just the beginning. The end of the proposal writing process is after the funding ends and all the reports are in. On time. And accurately.

It's important to remember that grants are legal contracts, and your organization takes on the additional role, and the duties, of a trustee. Your organization is bound to perform by the terms described in the grant.

Remember that foundations have legal obligations, too. You are the vehicle for fulfilling those obligations. That's why it's so important to communicate changes as soon as possible to funders. It's not because they like being sticklers. It's because foundations are held legally liable for their decisions. They need time to adjust to any changes in terms of the contract, just as you do.

That's why it's so important, as well, to develop grant proposals in a group with program manager, finance officer, and grant writer input. You, as the fundraiser, make the ask, develop the relationship with the foundation, and report back to it.

Program managers need to fulfill the terms of the grant. As a legal contract, you better be sure program staff can do what you say they can do. And you only know that by asking them. Are your program goals realistic and achievable? Only someone intimately involved with implementing and managing the program will know that information. Don't overpromise deliverables to get the money—your program manager will hate you for it, you will probably fail in meeting grant objectives, and the foundation will be ticked off. Not worth it. Never overpromise.

And you need finance officers to tell you how much it will cost. It's your finance person who can compare your grant budget to the agency's chart of accounts to make sure all costs are covered, both direct and indirect. It's your finance person with the information on fringe benefits and square footage rental costs. It's your finance person who can tell you what financial reports are possible and what are not. The last thing in the world you want to do is get grant funding that costs more for your agency to administer than what it receives. If that's the case, walk away. It's your finance person who can let you know when the grant means losing money.

If you don't already, I suggest you develop an ad hoc working group consisting of you, a program manager, and a finance director to provide input into developing proposals and writing grant requests. It will pay off in spades.

So, research, research, research. Like individuals, appeal to the foundation's values and needs. Be mission focused. Pay attention to the details. Communicate authentically and courteously. Acknowledge the foundation and its contributions, even if you don't get the funding. Make a good impression. You never know—it may lead to future funding, or another source of funding.

Wrapping It Up

- Like individuals, foundations are interested in mission fulfillment.
- Foundations are legally bound in their giving, and grant awards are legal contracts. Also, the grant recipient receives the money as a trustee over the funds.
- Examine a foundation's 990 before submitting an application.
- Details count.
- Develop proposals with input from finance officers and program managers.

Chapter Six

Building Relationships with Businesses

I n the last two chapters, we talked about building relationships with individuals and foundations. In this chapter, we address building donor relationships with businesses.

Like with individuals and foundations, relationships with businesses and corporate giving partners are not about you or your organization. They're about *them* and *their* needs, wants, and preferences. And they're still about impact. Only this time, they're not only about mission impact; they're also about financial and market impact.

Unlike individuals and private foundations, businesses are not obligated to give away money. Business owners are in it to make money. Corporations are accountable to stockholders who demand they make money. Never forget, no matter how charitable they may be, for-profit business donors and corporate giving partners have skin in the game because they believe their relationship with you will result in higher profits.

So how does a mission-oriented, socially accountable nonprofit help a for-profit business increase its profits?

Tapping into Business Contributions

The first and easiest way to increase your business partners' profits is by exposing business donors to new customers. If you have access to a large pool of people, be it staff, volunteers, clients, or individual donors who have some of the same characteristics as their typical customer, the business community may be interested in supporting you financially. They want awareness and exposure. Think of a business fundraising strategy where the companies can be exposed to a large audience of potential customers —exposure through a fundraising event, newsletter, press release, website, social media post, or volunteer of staff training, to name a few. Know how to measure your reach and effectively communicate results.

In addition to new customers, business partners are interested in increasing customer loyalty. They want people to buy their products or services again and again. They also want their customers to say good things about them and recommend them. They are keenly interested in their reputations in the community. This is where your mission comes in. By partnering with you, the company can be seen as doing good in the community. Which increases customer loyalty. Which ultimately helps sales, a for-profit's primary objective.

To capitalize on this motivation, think in terms of repeating opportunities for them and ways for you to craft your message in terms of community value, just like you would do with your individual donors. Remember, it's an exchange relationship. In addition to money, you're going to get a lot of PR and exposure to a new, potential donor base.

Business and corporate giving partners are also interested in decreasing their costs as much as they can. And not just the advertising costs associated with creating awareness and increasing exposure. Personnel costs probably take a big chunk of their budgets. Recent studies have shown that in addition to customer loyalty, perception of a company doing good in the community leads to lower employee recruitment and retention costs. This is why business philanthropy programs include employee giving matching gifts, company foundations, employee donor-advised funds, and employee volunteer opportunities.

Employee volunteer opportunities are also an excellent way to reduce a company's employee training costs—employees learn and practice many leadership and soft skills through volunteering. To get more out of your business donor relationships, think in terms of offering monthly-giving programs, matching-gift opportunities, and meaningful volunteer experiences.

Companies may also be looking for opportunities to access legislators and governmental regulatory agency staff. What connections do you have with legislators and government officials? Who do you invite to your events? Who comes? What other networking opportunities does your nonprofit put on that will offer business executives access to the regulators they want to influence?

Establishing Credibility with Business Donors

You gain credibility with individual donors mainly through your website and word of mouth. According to the Blackbaud Institute, 64 percent of individual donors research an organization through its website. Foundations conduct their background research mainly through the attachments you send them, usually an audit, 990, board list, IRS determination letter, and maybe some marketing materials.

Foundations want to make sure that the organization they are giving to will be around for a while and has the capacity to administer their contribution. When you ask for money from individuals and foundations, you only need a basic knowledge and understanding of your agency's financial statements to get donations.

Not true when working with business donors. With businesses, your fundraising strategy must be different than other donor groups. For-profits are keenly interested in your agency's financial performance. As a fundraiser, you need to intimately know your agency's financial performance to get the most from the corporate giving relationship. Being able to speak to your agency's financial health puts you heads and shoulders above the rest. You need to be able to talk about assets and liabilities, return on investment, profit margin, debt ratio, and growth trends—financially, as well as programmatically.

If you don't know how to read and interpret your agency's financials, find out how. Read a book. Find a webinar. Go to a training. Anything that will help you to talk in terms of financial, as well as mission, performance, will pay off. One book Joanne wrote, *Succeed in Your Nonprofit Funding Relationships: Analyzing Their Costs and Benefits,* published by CharityChannel Press, may help.

Another area of performance business donors are keenly interested in, and typical fundraising staff usually have limited knowledge of, is agency market performance. What is your reputation, or brand, in the community? How do you know? Do you have evidence to back up your claims? What markets, other than clients, do you serve? Think staff, donors, advocates, and collaborators, in addition to clients. What services and benefits do you provide to each of those markets? What is your market position in each group? What is your reach? How do you know? What evidence do you have? Who are your competitors? How do you differentiate from them? What makes you unique? What is your case for support? Linda's course and book, *Raise More Money from Your Business Community* covers how to present your case to businesses.

These are the kinds of questions that business and corporate giving partners are going to be interested in. The good news is that if you're doing research on and getting feedback from your individual donors, you're halfway there. Your human resources department may conduct employee surveys and have other employee group information. Your executive director or chief operations manager may have information on collaborative agency partnerships. Or you may already have it for grant narratives. You may also have a case for support from previous fundraising campaigns. Leverage what you're already doing.

Many strategies will interest business partners in making a contribution to your organization. In addition to the common event sponsorships, you can integrate agency communication activities with your government fundraising strategy. You can provide networking opportunities. Be creative and offer them ways to interact with all your organizational markets— staff, donors, advocates, clients, and community partners. Know your organization's market and financial performance to get top dollar. Get training where you need it. Leverage your existing efforts. Help businesses meet their goals. And watch them respond with donations to you.

Wrapping It Up

- Always remember a business's primary purpose is to make money.
- Know your agency's financial position inside and out.
- Be able to speak to your organization's market performance.
- Companies have more than money to give away.

Chapter Seven

Building Relationships with Government Funders

W e've previously discussed building relationships with individual donors, foundations, and businesses. We now turn our attention to building relationships with government funders.

Let's start with what's the same.

Just like with other types of donors, a relationship with a government funder is an exchange relationship. Each partner gets something out of it. Each partner can get their objective met through a relationship with the other partner. It's *still* not about you or your organization, it's about them and their needs, wants, and preferences. You need to know and speak to their values, needs, and motivations. You need to research them. Thoroughly. Like other institutional funders, they will be interested in your financial health. They want to make sure you can programmatically and financially handle a government contract and that your organization will be around for a while. They will also be interested in the extent of your reach in the community.

And know, like other institutional donors, government funders will be interested in data. Back up your claims with data.

So, what's different?

Building relationships with government funders is very different than building relationships with individuals, foundations, and businesses in that in building government relationships, you have two distinct groups to reach: the legislators who make the laws that provide and allocate the funding and the government employees who enforce the rules of the legislation.

To effectively communicate with government officials, both elected and employed, you research them differently than individuals, foundations, and businesses. The word "mission" needs to be interpreted slightly differently when dealing with the government than with other types of donors. And the motivations of legislators and government employees are very different than those of individuals, foundations, or businesses. In other words, your government fundraising strategy is different and more complicated than the fundraising strategies of other types of donors.

Let's talk about legislators first.

Building Relationships with Legislators

Legislators are in office because of one thing: voters put them there. And that is elected officials' primary objective: getting enough votes to stay in office. If you, as a fundraiser, want to get the attention of an elected official, talk about what's in the voters' minds. What's important to the community? What issues are important to community voting blocks? Who are your agency's constituencies? Not only the clients, but also the supporters, like the advocates, the donors, and the partner groups. How big a group are they? How influential are they? What is your reach with them? What is your influence with them? How are your agency's issues relevant to the public? How do addressing your agency's issues affect the community and the way it votes?

You, as a nonprofit, may not be able to lobby for specific candidates or legislation, but you can advocate for your cause and educate your legislators about community issues. And you can educate your community about legislative issues. Do you know what issues are important to your community? Have you asked them? Do you sit on community boards? Do you know what issues are coming up for a vote? Do you have communication channels you already have in place that you can leverage to educate your constituencies about community issues? Do you survey your clients, staff, volunteers, and donors? What are the voter's concerns? How do you know?

You also need to talk about mission, the public greater good. How do you talk to legislators about your agency's mission? Do you talk about the plight of your unfortunate clients, or do you talk about the opportunity to improve the community of the people who vote? Come from a position of strength, not weakness. Come from a perspective of "here is how we can work together in addressing community issues that are going to help me fulfill my mission and help you look good in the eyes of the voters."

Elected officials also need exposure. Do you offer any fundraising or networking events where they can speak to potential voters? What about your communication channels with clients, staff, volunteers, donors, and partner agencies—can you leverage them?

Do you leverage existing advocacy and communication activities as part of your government fundraising strategy? If not, you should.

Building Relationships with Government Employees

To be successful in getting government funding, you also must be aware of the employed staff: the program officers and their reports. If you got picked for government funding, the mission of your government-funded program is assumed to be the mission described in the legislation. It is assumed that the legislation and the regulations surrounding it are approved by a majority of the voters through their opportunities for public comment. It is the job of the government employees to enforce the will of the people as manifested in legislation and regulations. Government employees aren't in the game to get votes. They're in the game to carry out government funding according to the rules and regulations. It's up to the government staffers to implement the program as mandated by law.

Government employees are accountable to the elected officials, usually as part of a vast bureaucracy. Where they probably don't have much control. If you want to get along with a government employee, know all the rules and regulations and follow them. It will make the government employee's life easier. And relations with government funders will be easier.

But knowing all the rules and regulations associated with any particular governmental funding allocation is easier said than done. First of all, you need to know the legislation that determined the funding. And you need to know the legislation that law was built on. And the one before that. Sometimes, you need to go back to legislation that is decades old. It takes a lot of time and effort.

Then you need to know the regulations surrounding financial and program operations of the funding. The government has particular financial and programmatic restrictions that must be followed. And your agency will, sooner or later, be audited. If you don't pass the audit, you may have to return money that was already spent that you now don't have. Or you may be sanctioned and subject to harsher reporting requirements. Not to mention the PR nightmares that can ensue.

So next time that government employee gets on your case about whatever minor infraction you may have committed, thank your lucky stars that it's being called to your attention while it is fixable without severe consequences. You may be annoyed, but it may be saving your agency.

As part of your government fundraising strategy, leverage your current communication and fundraising activities. Invite government officials to networking events. Feature government funders in your communication channels. Survey your clients, staff, volunteers, donors, and advocates. Educate legislators about need in your community coming from the perspective of the voters in that community. Educate your community about critical legislative issues. Understand and be responsive to the needs of government employees. Research and research some more. Know their needs, wants, and perspectives. Make their lives easier, and they will return the favor.

Wrapping It Up

- Like building relationships with individuals, foundations, and businesses, building relationships with government funders is an exchange relationship.
- With government funders, you have two groups you need to reach: the legislators and the employed staff.
- Mission is assumed to be the same as the intent of the law.
- The legislators are in it for the votes. Government employees are in it for adherence to the rules and regulations.
- They both want to make sure you can handle a governmental priority and successfully implement funded legislation.

Chapter Eight

The Importance of Thanking Your Donors

All competent fundraisers know to thank their donors after donations come in. But how many fundraisers actually do it? Sadly, not many. Try making seven $10 donations to seven organizations new to you and see how many thank-you acknowledgments you get. Now count how many you get within three to five days of making your donation. Try it. See what happens.

According to the Fundraising Effectiveness Project, the first-year donor retention is a puny 23 percent. The overall donor retention rate is a still-poor 46 percent and has hovered around that level for years. Maybe the donor retention would be higher if more fundraisers would just meaningfully say *thank you* more promptly and more often.

Engaging and Retaining Your Donors by Saying Thank You

Saying thank you acknowledges and validates the actions someone has gone out of their way to do on your organization's behalf. As we discussed in **Chapter Four,** people want to be acknowledged and validated. Saying thank you meets a person's basic need to feel valued. And people appreciate having their needs met. People are much more likely to respond to your needs if you respond to theirs.

A simple thank you goes a long way toward building strong donor relationships. The donor has given. You have responded. Your response shows you are willing to engage in a two-way relationship. You already know the donor is invested enough in your agency's mission because of the donation. Build on that emotional investment. Take the next step to developing a successful donor relationship and ask your donor to do something besides making a donation. Ask the donor to follow you on

Facebook, take a survey, join you for an educational event—whatever it is, engage your donor. Increase the likelihood that you will retain your donors and they will give again. It all starts with that first thank you. Use saying thank you for engaging your donors in a two-way relationship.

To create the most effective donor relationships, thank your donors not only when they make a donation, but whenever they respond to a call to action. You can never thank your donors too often. I have never met any donor who was offended by being thanked too much unless the thank you came across as unauthentic. Let your donors know you and your nonprofit appreciate what they did. Acknowledge and validate them each time they contribute to your agency's mission, whether it be time, talent, or treasure. Create an ongoing positive cycle of donor engagement and mission fulfillment.

Meaningful messages lead to good feelings about your agency, creating good donor experiences. People are more likely to repeat positive experiences than neutral or negative ones. Meaningful messages are personal and authentic. A meaningful thank you is more than the automatic reply your website may generate or an impersonal communication from you about charitable deductions. A meaningful thank-you letter can have a handwritten message from the executive director or board member. Or send a personalized note about something that is happening in the donor's life. Or a letter from a service recipient can be included. If the donor is interested in a specific aspect of your organization, tailor your message's mission component to relate to that aspect. Do you know what your donors' interests are? Do you record your donors' preferences in your database? How up to date are your donor records? It is important to keep your donor records current and up to date for more than just financial purposes.

Deliver a thank you within forty-eight hours, while the memory of making the gift is still fresh in the donor's mind. Otherwise, your message is diluted, either because the donor doesn't remember making the donation or so much time has passed that your message comes across as perfunctory. If a thank you comes across as superficial, you just lost an opportunity to strengthen your relationship with the donor. Which is important because you engage donors through relationships.

Personal phone calls and emails from staff, board members, or service recipients can also be very meaningful to the donor. The fact that someone took time out of their busy day to make a personal phone call or write a personal message really shows the donors that you care and appreciate them.

Effective Donor Thank-You Letters Emphasize Fulfillment of Mission, not Financial Need

Mention mission fulfillment when you thank your donors. As we saw in **Chapter One,** it is mission, not money, that motivates. So, relate the act of giving to meeting mission in your thanking—just as much as in your asking. People want to be a part of something bigger than themselves. Their acts of donating money to you just gave your organization resources to do that. So, in addition to the monetary amount, make sure you mention mission impact when you thank your donors. Give them feedback on the results of their actions. Let them feel that they are crucial to mission impact. It is an easy way to keep your donors motivated.

Talking about your mission also gives donors fuel to become ambassadors for your agency. Wouldn't it be great if your current donors were recruiting new donors? How do you ask your donors to help you spread the word about your agency? Do you engage them in ways beyond donating money? If you do, watch those engaged donors stick around. And watch their gifts increase in frequency and size. With increased donor retention, more gifts, and more substantial average gifts, your fundraising performance will exponentially improve, garnering you more resources to fulfill more mission.

People appreciate being thanked. When they are thanked, people's efforts are acknowledged. They feel validated, which leads to goodwill. Talking about mission fulfillment motivates them to stay involved. Meaningful messages lead to even stronger goodwill. Thanking them often, after every call to action, further engages them. And higher donor engagement leads to better fundraising performance.

And better fundraising performance leads to more mission fulfillment. And mission fulfillment is what motivates your donors to get more involved and give again.

So, remember to thank your donors promptly and often.

Wrapping It Up

- A simple thank you goes a long way toward building positive donor relationships.
- Deliver a meaningful thank you within forty-eight hours of receiving a donation.
- Thank your donors after any call to action, including nonfinancial ones.
- When you thank, talk about mission, not financial, fulfillment.

Chapter Nine

Creating Donor Communications that Work

Engaging donors, in part, means creating a communications plan that develops two-way relationships. It's not only you talking to them, but it's also them talking to you, too. And it's not only them giving to you, but it's also you giving to them. It's a two-way street. To be a successful relationship, each party will give and get something as a result of the interaction. You want them to listen and respond to your request. If you want them to listen to you, you need to listen to them. If you want them to respond to you, you need to respond to them. If you want them to meet your needs, you must meet theirs first.

Effective Donor Communications Step One: Know Your Donors

Know your donors inside and out. Know their needs, values, and preferences. Understand their motivations for giving. Understand why they would welcome a communication from you.

It is not about you and what you need. It is not about why you think you're great or how their gift will help your organization. It's about them fulfilling their needs and values in ways they find satisfying. Frame your donor communications using *their* perspectives and interests. Get their attention in ways they are most likely to pay attention to and understand. Make it easy for them to notice you. Catch their attention by presenting concepts and images in ways that speak to them most strongly.

If you want to know your donors as a group, do your research. Go to the census bureau and get demographic data. Visit the Center for Generational Kinetics to find the global preferences of your different age cohorts. Look at the Giving USA, Charity Navigator, and Blackbaud Institute donor studies to see who's giving what to what. Google "communication trends" and read any number of articles about who likes to communicate how.

For specific donor information, keep good records when you interact with your donors. And review them regularly. *Recordkeeping is a must if you want to develop long-term relationships that show your donors you hear them and care enough to know and remember what they have to say.*

Effective Donor Communications Step Two: Get Their Attention

For donors to even notice you, you need to send them messages using communication channels they are most comfortable with. That means you probably will not text an eighty-year-old or send a direct mail piece to a twenty-something. However, don't presume that this is always the case. Many donors in their eighties are quite comfortable with social media and the Internet. Meet them on their turf. Find out, if you don't know, who likes letters, voice mails, emails, social media posts, or texts. Start the donor relationship sending the message, "Your preferences are important to me."

When you communicate, remember that you should not promote how great your organization is or how much your organization needs the money. Donors are more interested in mission and impact than they are organizational operations. Instead of talking about how their money helps you, address their interests, values, and needs. For example, there's a big difference between saying, "Last year demand for my organization's services grew 47 percent" or "Last year my organization fed five thousand people" and saying something like, "When was the last time you were hungry? How did it affect you?" Which one grabs more of your attention?

If you want donors to read your message, make it about them. Make it relatable. Make it emotionally appealing. Talk about them. Make the message about they can make an impact that is meaningful to them, not you or your organization.

If you're not sure what their interests, values, and needs are, ask them. You can survey your donors and ask for opinions. You can do it formally or informally. You can ask in person, or you can have a questionnaire. You can ask a large group of people, or you can ask a few influencers. There are many ways to conduct donor research. Just make sure that whatever response group you use is representative. And remember that for every group characteristic, there are individual exceptions.

And remember to record everything in your donor database.

Effective Donor Communications Step Three: Make it Personal

When you communicate with donors, do it in the second person. Make your message personally relatable. Use the words 'you' and 'your' liberally. Talk about what you (the donor) can accomplish, the impact you (the donor) are making. Make your donors the center of your mission fulfillment success. Let them know how important they are to mission success. Make them feel like they are the most influential people in the world in making the world a better place. In this way, you validate them and acknowledge them. And meet some of their primary emotional needs: the need to contribute to something bigger than themselves and doing something of worth. And they will find the interaction with you satisfying and thus will be more likely to continue and maybe strengthen the donor relationship.

Effective Donor Communications Step Four: Have a Call to Action

Now that you have their attention, engage your donors. Make your donor communications two-way interactions and give donors a way to respond to you. This means when you send them messages, using channels they are most comfortable with, you need to incorporate ways for them to respond to you. Ask them to do something. They can visit their legislators, vote, volunteer, sign up for an event, attend an event, invite a friend, donate money, contact you, fill out a survey, forward a message, and so on. Give them ways to make an impact on an issue they care about. Engage donors in your mission. Build those relationships.

Be clear—very, very clear—in your call to action. Be direct and be specific. And give a deadline.

Effective Donor Communications Step Five: Engage Them

When they respond to your request, reply back.

Let them know you know and appreciate what they did. Acknowledge and validate them again. Meet their emotional needs again. Build that strong donor relationship. Thank them. Give them feedback on the results of their actions. Let them feel like they are crucial to mission impact, again.

Then engage them some more. Send them another call to action. Create an ongoing positive cycle of donor engagement and mission fulfillment. Watch those engaged donors stick around. And watch the gifts from engaged donors increase in frequency and size. With increased donor retention, more gifts, and larger average gifts, your financial results will improve. Which will be poured into mission and increase mission fulfillment. Which you report back to your donors, making them the heroes. And you validate them again. And so on.

Effective Donor Communications Plan Step Six: Communicate Timely and Often

How often should you communicate with donors? Well, anytime you have a request to do something, and anytime they have responded to those requests. And mix up your requests. Don't make all your requests about donating money. You can send a survey. You can ask for feedback. You can get opinions. There are lots of things you can ask your donors to do that don't involve money.

When you make the call to action, give a deadline and respond immediately after that with an update. If you have asked them to contact you, call them back within twenty-four hours. If you have asked them to donate, they need to be thanked within forty-eight hours of your receiving their donation.

Believe me, most nonprofits don't do this. If you thank your donors within forty-eight hours of making a donation, you will catch their attention just because it's not the norm. If you have asked them to fill out a survey, let them know you have their feedback and are compiling results as soon as the survey ends. Then let them know when you're going to release the results. And then let them know the survey results.

If you have asked them to visit their legislators or vote or advocate in some other way, send periodic updates on where in the legislative process the issue stands. If you asked them to volunteer, sign up for an event, attend an event or invite a friend, give them updates on event attendance—integrated into how that translates into greater community impact, of course.

Know your donors inside and out. Use their preferred communication channels. Talk to them about things they are interested in ways that they will find satisfying. Ask them to do something. Give them a way to do it. And when they do it, respond back. Thank your donors. Report back to them. Dialog with them. Interact with your donors in ways meaningful for them. Engage your donors. Let them engage with you. Build a successful donor relationship. And watch your fundraising results soar.

Wrapping It Up

- Know your donors' needs, values, preferences, and motivations.
- Make your communications with donors personable and relatable. Use the words 'you' and 'your' liberally.
- After making a call to action, follow up by reporting results.
- Communicate timely and often.

Chapter Ten

Bringing It All Together

So, what have we learned about how to find new donors and keep them giving?

Relationship building is the crux of your fundraising success. Getting that donation is not about getting the money so much as it's about developing and keeping up a two-way relationship with the donor. No matter what kind of potential donor you're pursuing—individual, foundation, business, legislator, or government employee—you are in an exchange relationship where all parties are giving and receiving something of value to them. Call it the partnership paradigm. The donor and your nonprofit are partners in achieving their respective goals.

The ultimate goal is community impact. To recruit and retain that new donor, we must be mission focused. Add market focus when recruiting and reporting to business donors. From approaching a potential donor to thanking them, we must stay mission-centric and focus on community impact. Donors are not ATM's spitting out money. They want to make a difference. Show them how they can do that by making a financial contribution. Make your donor the hero in fulfilling your agency's mission.

Be donor-centric as much mission-centric. To do that, you need to know your donors' needs, values, preferences, and motivations. Thoroughly research potential donors. Look at the research findings available through the census bureau, Center for Generational Kinetics, and Blackbaud Institute. Examine the 990s. Know your nonprofit's financial and market positions. Know what's important to your donor before approaching them. And when you do contact them, contact them in ways meaningful to *them*. Talk to them about things *they* are interested in and in ways that they will find satisfying. Use *their* language. Meet *their* needs. Use *their* preferred communication channels. Let them know their goals are important to you. Make it possible for them to achieve their goals by giving to your organization.

A donor needs three things to be able to give to your organization: to be aware of and physically connected with your nonprofit, to have the ability to give, and to be invested in your agency in some way. To find new donors, ask the people who are already invested in your organization: board members, staff, volunteers, vendors, business partners, and business associations. They already have skin in the game and want you to succeed. Tell them how they can make an even bigger impact. Then look at your connections' connections. After that, turn to recruiting potential donors who don't have any connection to your agency but are interested in your cause. Don't just ask anybody. Target your efforts.

According to the Fundraising Effectiveness Project, the average overall nonprofit donor retention is 46 percent. The average first-time donor retention rate is a mere 23 percent. On average, it costs six times more to acquire as opposed to retain a new donor. The most cost-beneficial fundraising technique you can use to realize increased revenues is to improve your donor retention rate.

The number-one thing you can do to ensure that donors will give again is to thank them. People appreciate being thanked. When they are thanked, people's efforts are acknowledged, and they feel validated, which leads to goodwill. Deliver a meaningful thank you within forty-eight hours of receiving a donation. Thank donors seven to ten times through a variety of channels, over time. Show your donors the impact they made through their contributions. A simple thank you goes a long way toward building positive donor relationships. So, remember to thank your donors promptly and often.

When you thank your donors, talk about mission fulfillment, not financial needs. Talking about mission fulfillment motivates donors to stay involved.

Ask donors to become involved in ways other than making a donation. Ask them to share a post, forward an email, sign a petition, take a survey, volunteer, or invite a friend. Engage your donors. Engaged donors tend to give more frequently and more often. Thank your donors after any call to action. Thanking them regularly, after every call to action, further engages them. And higher donor engagement leads to better fundraising performance.

It's not only you talking to them, but it's them talking to you, too. You want them to listen and respond to your request, of course. But if you want them to listen to you, you need to listen to them. Ask questions. Listen to the answers. Feedback information. When asked questions, answer them. If you don't know the answer, find out, and get back to them. Return phone calls within forty-eight hours. If you want them to respond to you, then you need to respond to them. If you want them to meet your needs, you must meet theirs first. Engage your donors in a two-way relationship.

Your level of engagement with potential donors determines your success in getting them to give to your organization, not only once but again and again. Be a mission maven. Put your donors first. Build satisfying relationships. Go beyond money. Watch your donations grow.